LIFE
PROCESSES

Life Cycles

Holly Wallace

Heinemann Library
Chicago, Illinois

Designed by Celia Floyd
Originated by Dot Gradations
Printed by Wing King Tong, in Hong Kong

05 04 03 02 01

10 9 8 7 6 5 4 3 2 1

Library of Congress Cataloging-in-Publication Data

Wallace, Holly, 1961-
  Life Cycles / Holly Wallace.
      p. cm. -- (Life processes)
  Includes bibliographical references (p.).
  ISBN 1-57572-339-5 (library)
  1. Life cycles (Biology)--Juvenile literature. [1. Life cycles (Biology)] I. Title. II. Series.

  QH501 .G36 2000
  571.8--dc21

                                            00-040973

Acknowledgments

The author and publishers are grateful to the following for permission to reproduce copyright material: Corbis, p. 24; NHPA/ANT, p. 5; NHPA/G. I. Bernard, pp. 5, 7, 13; NHPA/N.A. Callow, p. 13; NHPA/Stephen Dalton, pp. 12, 13, 19; NHPA/Ron Fotheringham, p. 13; NHPA/Pavel German, p. 21; NHPA/Brian Hawkes, p. 8; NHPA/Stephen Krasemann, pp. 14, 15; NHPA/Gerard Lacz, p. 27; NHPA/Yves Lanceau, p. 26; NHPA/M. I. Walker, p. 4; Oxford Scientific Films/Doug Allan, p. 22; Oxford Scientific Films/Daniel J. Cox, p. 23; Oxford Scientific Films/Mark Deeble & Victoria Stone, p. 16; Oxford Scientific Films/Zig Leszczynski, p. 20; Oxford Scientific Films/Colin Milkins, p. 15; Planet Earth Pictures/Doug Perrine, p. 16; Robert Harding Picture Library/ Raj Kamal, p. 11.

Cover photograph reproduced with permission of Oxford Scientific Films.

Every effort has been made to contact copyright holders of any material reproduced in this book. Any omissions will be rectified in subsequent printings if notice is given to the publisher.

Some words are shown in bold, **like this.** You can find out what they mean by looking in the glossary.

Contents

Introduction

Life Cycles looks at the different stages in a living thing's life, from its birth through its growth and development. It also describes how living things care for their young. All living things eventually die, so they **reproduce** to replace themselves. Then the amazing cycle of life can begin again.

Living and Dying

A life cycle describes the main stages in the life of a living thing, such as birth, growth, **reproduction,** and death. Reproduction means the creation of new life. All living things reproduce in order to continue their **species,** and to replace those that die. They reproduce in two main ways, **asexual** reproduction and **sexual** reproduction.

Asexual reproduction

Asexual reproduction is the simplest form of reproduction. It happens in many simple animals and plants. In asexual reproduction, only one parent is needed. There are different types of asexual reproduction. The parent may simply split in two, or part of the parent may bud or split off to form a new individual. New individuals created in this way are always identical to their parents because they share the same **genetic** make-up.

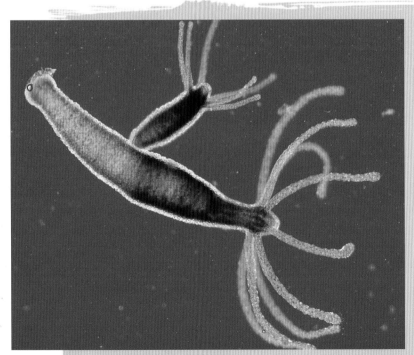

A hydra reproduces asexually by budding.

Hydra reproduction

Asexual reproduction is more common in plants than in animals, but some animals do reproduce this way. A hydra is a tiny, tentacled creature that lives in freshwater ponds. It can reproduce by budding. In budding, a group of cells grows on the hydra's stalk-like body, produces tentacles, then buds off its parent to form a new animal.

Sexual reproduction

All flowering plants and most animals reproduce sexually. In sexual reproduction, there are always two parents. Each parent makes sex cells called male and female **gametes,** and each carries half of the genetic material for the new individual. The two parents must join together to create a **zygote** in a process called **fertilization.** From the fertilized cell, a new living thing develops.

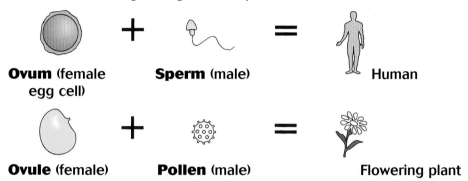

Ovum (female egg cell)   **+**   **Sperm** (male)   **=**   Human

Ovule (female)   **+**   **Pollen** (male)   **=**   Flowering plant

Strawberry plants reproduce sexually with seeds and asexually by putting out side stems called runners. The runners put down roots and grow into new plants.

Internal and external fertilization

Fertilization takes place either internally, inside the female's body, or externally, outside her body. In an example of external fertilization, the female crab sheds her egg cells in the sand on the shore or in shallow water. The male then fertilizes them with his sperm.

The fertilized eggs are washed out to sea, where they hatch into **larvae.**

A female crab releases her eggs into the sea.

Flowering Plants

Flowering plants reproduce by **sexual** reproduction. A plant's flowers contain the plant's male and female reproductive organs. New plants grow from seeds. For a seed to be produced, **pollen** must be transferred from the male parts of the plant to the female parts. This process is called **pollination.** Some plants self-pollinate, which means that they use their own supply of pollen. However, most cross-pollinate, which means that they need pollen from another plant to make their seeds. When pollination has happened, the flower dies.

Inside a Buttercup Flower

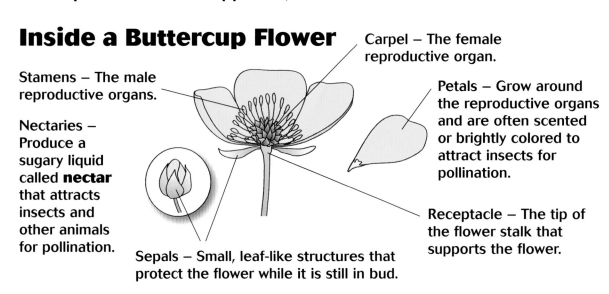

Carpel – The female reproductive organ.

Stamens – The male reproductive organs.

Nectaries – Produce a sugary liquid called **nectar** that attracts insects and other animals for pollination.

Petals – Grow around the reproductive organs and are often scented or brightly colored to attract insects for pollination.

Receptacle – The tip of the flower stalk that supports the flower.

Sepals – Small, leaf-like structures that protect the flower while it is still in bud.

The carpel is made up of an ovary, a stigma, and a style. The ovary contains tiny **ovules,** the female sex cells. The stigma catches the pollen grains. The style joins the stigma to the ovary.

Stigma

Style

Ovary

Ovule

A stamen is made up of a filament and an anther. The anther produces pollen grains, the male sex cells. The filament holds the anther up to be pollinated.

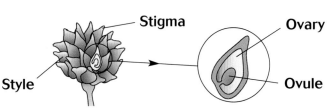

Filament

Anther

Pollen

Pollen transfer

For a seed to grow, pollen must be transferred from the male to the female parts of a flower. The anther splits open, releasing millions of tiny pollen grains. Once a grain lands on the female stigma, it grows a long tube that reaches down the style and into the ovary. The pollen grain has two **nuclei.** One joins with the nucleus of the egg cell inside the ovule to form a new cell. The other joins with two other cells in the ovule to form a store of food.

Did you know?

Plants have a variety of life spans. Some flowering plants, called **annuals,** live for only a year. They grow, quickly produce their flowers and seeds, and then die. **Perrenials** are plants that live for many years. They die at the end of each growing season, but grow new shoots at the start of the next.

Flower designs

Flowers rely on the wind and animals, such as insects, birds, and bats, to transfer their pollen. A flower's shape, color, and smell is determined by how it is pollinated. Wind-pollinated flowers, such as grass flowers, are small and drab because they do not need to attract pollinating animals. Insect-pollinated flowers have bright petals, sweet smells, and a store of sugary nectar to tempt butterflies and bees. The insects visit the flowers to drink their nectar, and become coated in pollen, which they carry to the next flower they visit.

Honeybees help with pollination.

From Seeds to Plants

Once the **pollen** has **fertilized** the **ovule,** the ovule grows into a seed. The seed contains the beginnings of a new plant and a store of food for the plant to use until it grows leaves and can make food for itself. The ovary develops into a protective fruit around the seed. The fruit may be a nut, berry, or pod. The seed must travel away from the parent plant to avoid competition for light and space and find a suitable place to grow. The process by which a seed produces its first root and shoot, and begins to grow into a new plant is called **germination.** The main parts of a seed are shown here.

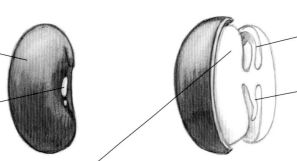

Testa – The protective casing around the seed.

Hilum – The scar on the seed, showing where the ovule was attached to the ovary.

Plumule – The plant's first shoot.

Radicle – The plant's first root.

Cotyledon or seed leaf – Food for the new plant is stored in the cotyledons. Some seeds have two cotyledons (dicotyledons, such as daisies and poppies). Others have one (monocotyledons, such as daffodils and grasses).

Seed dispersal

Many plants rely on wind, water, birds, and animals to disperse their seeds. Dandelion seeds are very light. They are attached to tiny, fluffy parachutes and are easily blown in the wind. Birds eat fleshy fruits, such as berries or rosehips. The seeds, or pips, pass through their bodies and are dispersed with their droppings. Burdock fruits are covered in tiny hooks that catch on to the fur of animals.

This diagram shows how a seed germinates.

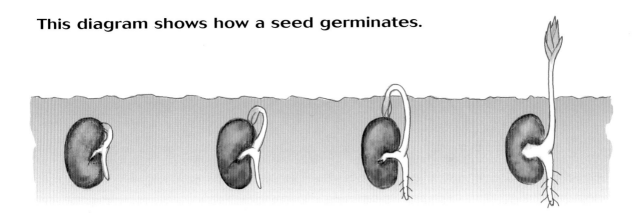

1. The seed takes in water and swells up. Chemicals inside the seed convert the starchy food store into **glucose,** which the seed needs for growth.

2. A few days later, the radicle pushes through the testa into the soil. Root hairs absorb water and minerals from the soil.

3. The plumule grows upwards through the soil. It is hooked so it can push through the soil without damaging the growing tip.

4. Soon the plant grows its first leaves and begins to make food by **photosynthesis.**

Conifer life cycles

Conifers have cones instead of flowers or fruit. Each cone is either male or female. Male pollen cells are carried to female cones to fertilize the female cells and produce seeds. The seeds are protected inside the cones, which harden and turn brown. When the weather is warm and dry, the cones open up and release the seeds. The seeds have tiny wings for floating on the breeze.

Bristlecone pine cones.

Growing from Spores

Some plants do not reproduce from seeds. They produce microscopic, dust-like specks of living material, called **spores.** Millions of spores are released into the air and carried away by the wind. If they find a suitable place to grow, they will develop into new plants. Plants that reproduce with spores include ferns, mosses, horsetails, and liverworts. **Fungi** also reproduce with spores.

Fern life cycles

Ferns produce spores on the undersides of their fronds, in structures called **sporangia.** These are arranged in groups and often look like tiny patches of rust. When the spores are ripe, the sporangia open and release them into the air. Even if a spore lands in a good spot, it does not grow directly into a new fern. Ferns have two stages to their life cycles. The first is **asexual,** and the second is **sexual.**

The Life Cycle of a Fern

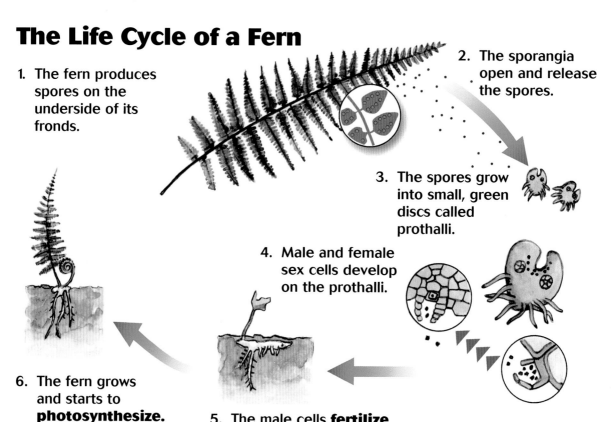

1. The fern produces spores on the underside of its fronds.

2. The sporangia open and release the spores.

3. The spores grow into small, green discs called prothalli.

4. Male and female sex cells develop on the prothalli.

5. The male cells **fertilize** the female cells, which grow into new fern plants.

6. The fern grows and starts to **photosynthesize.** Then it begins to produce its own spores.

How fungi reproduce

Fungi do not have flowers, leaves, proper roots, or stems. They do not have **chlorophyll** and cannot photosynthesize. Fungi used to be classified as plants, but they now form their own, separate kingdom. Like ferns, fungi reproduce with spores. The spores of mushrooms and toadstools grow under the cap, on ridges called **gills.** The cap protects the gills from rain while the stalk holds them up so that they can fall easily and catch the breeze.

Did you know?

Fungi produce huge numbers of spores. Giant puffballs, like the one in the picture, can measure up to 46 inches (116 centimeters) across, but more usually they measure about the same as a large melon. They can produce an incredible 70 billion spores, which they puff out in thick clouds. Puffballs do not have gills, but burst open to release their spores.

How a Toadstool grows

1. A spore lands on the ground and starts to **germinate.**

2. It grows into a mass of underground feeding threads, called *hyphae,* which form a structure called a button.

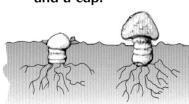

3. The button grows upwards. Its outer skin splits to show a stalk and a cap.

4. The stalk grows taller, and the cap expands to uncover its gills. The gills begin to produce spores. The whole process may only take a few hours.

11

Insect Life Cycles

Most insects hatch from eggs laid by the female. Only a very few types, such as aphids, produce live young. Most insects go through amazing series of changes as they develop from eggs into adults. This process is called **metamorphosis.** An adult insect's life may be very short. An adult mayfly, for example, only lives for one day. But during that time, the insect must find a mate and lay her eggs. There are two kinds of metamorphosis, complete and incomplete.

Complete metamorphosis

Some insects, such as moths, butterflies, bees, and beetles, go through complete metamorphosis. The newly-hatched young look very different from the adults. They change from eggs into **larvae,** then into **pupae,** before emerging as adults. On the next page you can follow the metamorphosis of a large white butterfly.

Incomplete metamorphosis

Some insects, such as locusts, grasshoppers, and dragonflies, go through incomplete metamorphosis. The young look similar to adults. They develop from eggs into **nymphs,** then into adults. Below you can follow the metamorphosis of a desert locust.

Locust life cycle

1. The locust lays her eggs in the sand. They take about ten days to hatch.

2. The eggs hatch into young called nymphs. These look like adult locusts, except that they do not have wings.

3. The nymphs feed and grow. Like all insects, locusts have to shed, or **molt,** their hard skins in order to grow. Locusts do this five times as they grow.

4. During the fifth molt, shown at left, an adult locust emerges, complete with wings.

Butterfly life cycle

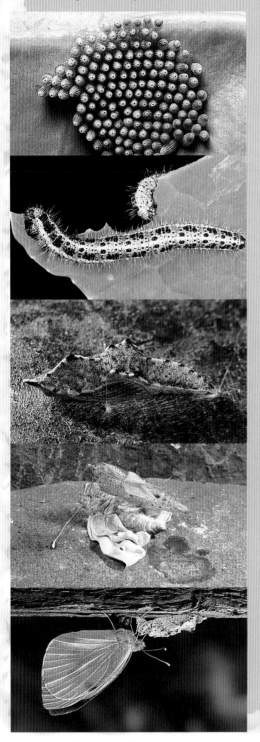

1. A female butterfly lays her barrel-shaped eggs on a cabbage leaf. They take about a week to hatch.

2. The eggs hatch into caterpillars, or butterfly larvae. They spend their time feeding on the cabbage leaves and growing.

3. Each caterpillar spins a silk **chrysalis** around its body and hangs underneath a cabbage leaf. It becomes a pupa inside the chrysalis, and starts to metamorphose.

4. Inside the chrysalis, the caterpillar's body is broken down. New organs and tissue grow to form an adult butterfly.

5. About three weeks later, the chrysalis splits open and an adult butterfly struggles out. Blood flows into its soft wings, making them rigid and ready for flight.

Did you know?

Most female insects lay their eggs and then abandon them, but female earwigs are caring mothers. They lay their eggs in a hole in the ground and stand guard over them. They wash them often to keep them free from **parasites.** Even when the eggs hatch, the mothers protect the young until they can look after themselves.

Spiders and Scorpions

Spiders and scorpions belong to a group of animals called arachnids. Their young, like those of insects, hatch from eggs. The eggs are **fertilized** inside the mother's body. When the **nymphs** hatch, they look like miniature versions of their parents. Then they **molt** several times before they reach adult size. Ticks and mites are also arachnids.

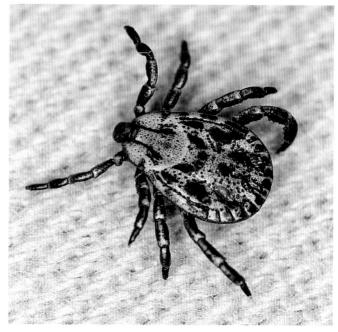

A rocky mountain tick is an arachnid.

Adult arachnids have eight legs. Newly-hatched ticks and mites have only six. They develop two more legs as they molt and grow. The life span of arachnids ranges from a few weeks in some types of mite to 30 years in some large spiders.

Dancing scorpions

Before they mate, some scorpions perform an elaborate courtship dance. First the male waves his pinchers in the air, taps his feet on the ground, and shakes his body to attract a female. Then the male and female link pinchers and move to and fro for hours on end. The eggs are fertilized inside the female's body.

Scorpions and young

The female scorpion lays up to 95 eggs. The eggs hatch almost at once. Then the baby scorpions climb up their mother's pinchers and on to her back. Their mother carries them around safe from predators until they have molted for the first time, and are able to fend for themselves.

14

Spider eggs

Because so many spider eggs die or are eaten, most spiders produce huge numbers of eggs to make sure that some survive. Cave spiders lay a single egg, but other spiders lay up to 2,500 at a time. The eggs are protected in a silk sac, or purse. Some kinds of spider guard and protect their eggs, while others leave them alone.

Spider care

After mating, the female wolf spider spins a silk purse around her eggs. The case remains attached to her spinnerets, silk-producing glands on her **abdomen.** When the female goes out hunting, she drags the purse with her. When the baby spiders hatch, she carries them on her back until they can look after themselves.

This female wolf spider is carrying her young on her back.

Did you know?

Horseshoe crabs are not crabs at all, but close relations of arachnids. They are found in warm seas. The crabs spend most of their lives on the seafloor, searching for worms and clams to eat. But every spring, at high tide, hundreds of thousands gather on the shore to mate and lay their eggs in the sand. The young are only about one inch (2.5 centimeters) long when they hatch. On their risky dash to the sea, many are eaten by birds.

15

Fish Life Cycles

Most fish lay their eggs, or **spawn,** in water. In many fish, **fertilization** takes place outside the female's body. The female lays her eggs in the water, and then the male covers them with his **sperm.** Some fish lay huge numbers of eggs. For example, a cod may lay six million eggs that float to the surface. The eggs contain a supply of food for the growing babies, and are also a nourishing source of food for birds and other fish. Many are eaten before they hatch, and others are not fertilized. Laying a large number of eggs is a way of making sure that at least some survive. Other fish, including some sharks, give birth to live young.

Lemon sharks give birth to live babies.

Did you know?

Most female fish lay their eggs, then leave them unattended. But some cichlid fish, called mouthbreeders, take great care to protect their young. The eggs are fertilized, then the females keep them in their mouth for ten days or so until they hatch. Even then, the young fish stay close to their mother and swim back into her mouth if danger threatens.

16

The emperor cichlid is a mouthbreeder.

Salmon life cycle

Most fish spend their whole lives either in the ocean or in freshwater. Salmon spend time in both. A salmon hatches and dies in the same stretch of fast-flowing river. But, in between, it makes an extraordinary journey out to sea to feed and grow into an adult. Below you can follow the salmon's life cycle.

Flatfish features

When young, a flatfish, such as a sole or flounder, is the same shape as most ordinary fish. But a few weeks after it hatches, it begins to change shape. One eye moves around to the other side of its head so that both eyes are on the same side. After about six weeks, its body is completely flat. It sinks to the seabed to lie on its blind side. Here it is perfectly **camouflaged** in the stones and sand.

1. The female salmon lays up to 5,000 eggs in a river. They are fertilized by several males.

2. The eggs hatch into tiny fish called alevins. They carry a pouch of food that will last for several weeks.

3. The alevins grow into fry. The fry grow into smolts.

6. After spawning, the adults die. Then the life cycle begins again.

4. After spending between one and five years in fresh water, the smolts swim out to sea to feed and grow. They travel thousands of miles in a journey that lasts for several years.

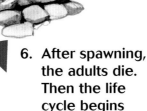

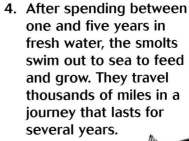

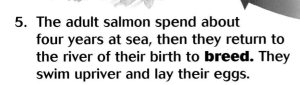

5. The adult salmon spend about four years at sea, then they return to the river of their birth to **breed.** They swim upriver and lay their eggs.

17

Amphibian Life Cycles

Amphibians are animals such as frogs, toads, and salamanders that are born in water, but spend most of their adult lives on land. Amphibians return to the water only to lay their eggs. Their name comes from the Greek word *amphibios,* and means "having two lives." At first, young amphibians are adapted to life in water. They breathe through **gills,** like fish, and have tails for swimming. Later, they develop features such as lungs and legs to help them survive on land. These changes are called **metamorphosis.**

Frog life cycle

Here you can follow the life cycle of a typical frog.

1. In spring, adult frogs arrive at a pond. The males croak loudly to attract females.

2. As the frogs mate, the females lay over 2,000 eggs to be **fertilized** by the males. The eggs, or **spawn,** are covered in jelly for protection. They float near the surface of the pond.

3. About two weeks later, the eggs hatch into tiny tadpoles that breathe through gills, taking in **oxygen** from the water.

4. Over the next three months, the tadpoles develop lungs and legs. Their tails shrink and they look like tiny frogs.

5. The froglets spend more and more of their time out of the water, then leave the pond completely. It takes three years for them to be fully grown. In the wild, frogs have many enemies, and their lives may be short. In captivity, however, frogs may live for up to ten years.

Caring parents

Some amphibians look after their eggs very carefully. Male midwife toads wrap strings of eggs around their back legs and carry them around with them. When the eggs are ready to hatch, the male goes to the pond and lowers his back legs into the water so that the tadpoles can swim away. The male Darwin's frog swallows his tadpoles and carries them in his throat. When they grow into froglets, he spits them out!

Breeding in water

In spring, frogs and toads go to a pond or lake to breed. Many return to the same breeding site year after year, often the same pond they were born in. They may travel several miles to reach their home pond, crossing dangerous roads and railways. They seem to use landmarks and their sense of smell to find their way. But they may also be guided by magnetism in the earth.

Did you know?

The odd-looking axolotl is a species of salamander from Mexico. Like other salamanders, axolotls start life as tadpoles, or **larvae,** with feathery gills. Scientists have discovered that axolotls need the chemical **iodine** to complete their life cycles and turn into adults. Unfortunately, there is no iodine in their natural **habitat.** This means that the axolotls never mature, although they become **fertile,** and are able to reproduce while still larvae.

Reptile Life Cycles

Reptiles, which include snakes, turtles, crocodiles, and lizards, lay their eggs on land. Reptile eggs have thick shells to keep them from drying out. Inside the eggs is everything the young reptiles need to develop, including food, water, and **oxygen.** Lizards and snakes lay eggs with flexible, leathery shells. Crocodiles lay eggs with hard shells. Some reptiles, especially those that live in cool places, produce live young. If they didn't, the eggs might become too cold and the young inside might die. Many reptiles lay their eggs in nests dug in the sand or soil or built out of leaves and stems.

Snake life cycle

The the main stages in the life cycle of an American corn snake are shown below.

1. The female lays her eggs in a rotten tree stump.
2. Inside its egg, the young snake feeds on the **yolk** and grows. It spends about eight weeks **incubating.**
3. The snake cuts a slit in the eggshell, using its egg tooth, the sharp piece of bone on its snout.
4. It spends the day in its shell, poking its head in and out.
5. The next day, it slithers out of the egg through another hole and off into the wild.
6. A few days later, it **molts** for the first time to allow it to grow. It will do this several more times until it reaches adult size.

A corn snake coiled protectively around its eggs.

Crocodile care

Crocodiles are caring parents. The female lays her eggs in a hole near the water's edge. She covers it with plants and soil to hide it from **predators.** She guards the nest for about three months, until the eggs hatch. When she hears a squeaking noise coming from the eggs, she knows it is time to dig them up. The baby crocodiles use their egg teeth to break out of their shells. Then their mother picks them up in her mouth and carries them to the water. The babies stay close to their mother until they are about two years old.

Dash to the sea

Sea turtles spend most of their lives in the ocean, but the females come ashore to lay their eggs. Some sea turtles swim thousands of miles from their feeding grounds to their nesting sites. They mate offshore, then the females dig a hole in the sand, lay their eggs, and return to the ocean. The newly-hatched turtles dig themselves out of the sand, then face a dangerous journey to the ocean. Many are eaten by crabs and predatory birds.

A newly-hatched green turtle heads for the safety of the sea.

Did you know?

Reptiles usually live for a long time. Small snakes may live for up to twelve years, larger snakes for 40 years or longer. But the longest-living reptile, and the longest-living land animal of all, is the huge Marion's tortoise. A male Marion's tortoise was believed to be more than 152 years old when it was killed, accidentally, in 1918.

Bird Life Cycles

A female bird lays eggs with hard shells. The eggs are **fertilized** inside her body. Most birds build nests to provide safe places to lay their eggs and to raise their young. During the **incubation period,** the eggs must be kept warm if they are to develop properly and hatch into healthy chicks. One parent, usually the female, sits on the eggs, holding them against the **brood patch** on its breast. Some eggs take about ten days to hatch, while others take as long as two months. Birds are caring parents. They stay with their chicks and bring them food until the chicks have learned to fly and can find food for themselves.

Birds' eggs

A bird's egg contains everything a young bird needs to survive and grow. Its hard shell gives protection but is covered with tiny holes that let **oxygen** in. The white of the egg, or **albumen,** contains water for the young bird. The **yolk** is its food supply. When the chick is fully developed, it cracks the shell open with its bony egg tooth and struggles out.

The male emperor penguin incubates the egg between its feet.

Penguin parents

Emperor penguins nest on the Antarctic ice in temperatures of -140°F (-45°C). The female lays a single egg, then swims off to sea to feed. The male cradles the egg in the warm space between his feet and his feathered belly, where it is protected by a flap of skin. He spends about three months in the freezing cold, without eating and hardly moving, until the egg hatches. Then the female returns to feed the chick.

Growing up

Different types of birds mature at different rates. Some young birds, such as goslings and ducklings, leave the nest almost immediately, although they still stay close to their parents. Others, such as pigeons and woodpeckers, are born blind and helpless. Their parents have to feed them constantly. Birds learn to fly at different times, too. A baby sparrow can fly within a day of hatching from its egg, whereas it takes a wandering albatross about nine months to make its first flight from its nest. Up until the time it takes its first flight it relies totally on its parents for food and protection.

An albatross on its nest with its chick.

Did you know?

In the wild, most small birds live for only about two to five years. Larger birds live longer, perhaps up to 30 years. But most wild birds do not die of old age. Millions are killed by **predators,** such as foxes and rats, or by cars. Others starve when food is scarce, or die from disease. Altogether, about three-quarters die before they are six months old. The longest-living birds are thought to be wandering albatrosses, which may live for about 80 years.

Mammal Life Cycles

Mammals are the group of animals that include human beings, dogs, whales, and cats. Mammals range in size from huge whales and elephants to tiny shrews and bats. Mammals reproduce **sexually,** and are the only animals that produce milk to feed their young. They feed and care for their young until they are old enough to fend for themselves. Most mammals give birth to live young that develop inside their mothers' bodies, after female egg cells have been **fertilized** by male **sperm.** But two special types of mammals, the **monotremes** and the **marsupials,** have more unusual life cycles.

Egg-laying mammals

Monotremes are very unusual mammals. There are three **species**—the duck-billed platypus, the long-beaked echidna, and the short-beaked echidna. The echidnas are also known as spiny anteaters. Monotremes are the only mammals that lay eggs. The platypus lays two soft, leathery eggs in a nest in a riverbank burrow. An echidna lays a single egg, which it carries in a small pouch underneath its body. When the egg hatches, the baby feeds on its mother's milk. The milk oozes on to the mother's fur, and the young animal laps it up.

The short-beaked echidna lays eggs.

Kangaroo life cycle

Marsupials are mammals with pouches, including koalas, kangaroos, and opossums. The females have pocket-like pouches on their stomachs. As with other marsupials, a new-born kangaroo, or joey, is tiny, blind, and helpless. It has to develop inside its mother's pouch before it can fend for itself. Below you can follow a kangaroo's life cycle.

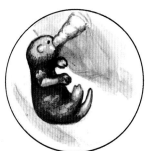

1. At birth, the baby kangaroo is only about an inch long. It crawls up its mother's fur and into her pouch.

2. Inside the pouch, it attaches itself to one of her teats. It starts to drink its mother's milk and to grow.

3. The joey begins to look more like a kangaroo. After about six months, it leaves the pouch for the first time, but soon hops back inside.

4. When it is about nine months old, it leaves the pouch for good. By this time, another joey may already be suckling inside. A kangaroo lives for 15 to 20 years.

Did you know?

The Virginia opossum has the shortest pregnancy of any mammal. It lasts for a maximum of thirteen days and can be as short as eight days. The baby opossum spends another four to five weeks developing inside its mother's pouch. The opossum also has the most young—about 20 babies in a single litter.

Placental Mammals

Mammals that are neither **monotremes** nor **marsupials** are called **placental** mammals. Their young grow and develop inside the mothers' bodies until they are fully formed. A baby placental mammal is born looking like a smaller version of its parents. **Fertilization** takes place internally, then the baby develops inside its mother's uterus, or womb. The baby gets **oxygen** and nourishment from its mother, through a spongy layer of cells called the placenta. In the placenta, the mother's blood supply lies close to that of the baby. Food and oxygen pass from the mother's blood into the baby's blood, and waste products pass from the baby to the mother.

A mare suckles its foal on milk.

Blue whale babies

Sea mammals, such as whales and dolphins, are born tail first. To stay alive, they must come to the surface to breathe air. Being born tail first keeps them from drowning as they are being born. The babies are pushed to the surface by their mother to take their first breath.

Blue whales have the largest babies of any mammal. At birth, a blue whale calf is already four to nine feet (1.3 to 3 meters) long and weighs three to four tons. It drinks a small bathtub-full of its mother's milk each day. By the time it is weaned at seven months old, a blue whale calf can weigh up to 20 tons. Blue whales can live for up to 65 years.

Batty nurseries

Each year, millions of free-tailed bats fly from Mexico to Texas to have their young. The young are raised inside cave nurseries, where they are warm and safe from **predators.** The caves are dark and very crowded. Bracken Cave contains some ten million baby bats. At night, the females leave the cave to search for food. When they return, they are able to find their own baby in the crowd by recognizing its particular call and smell.

Baby faces

All mammals look after their young, but the length of care varies from a few weeks in mice to several years in apes. A baby mammal's appearance is designed to show that it needs to be looked after. A baby orangutan, for example, is small, with big eyes and jerky movements. This sends a message to adult orangutans that it needs to be cared for.

An orangutan baby with its mother.

Did you know?

The shortest-lived mammal is the tiny shrew. In the wild the shrew lives for only 12 to 18 months. It is born one year, breeds the next, then dies. The elephant has the longest lifespan of all mammal animals. The oldest on record was an elephant called Raja, who died in captivity at the age of 82. In the wild, many Asian elephants live to be 55 to 70 years old.

Human Life Cycles

Like whales, orangutans, and bats, human beings are **placental** mammals. A human baby develops inside its mother until it is ready to be born. Then the mother feeds it on milk and takes care of it. Human beings care for their young longer than any other mammals do.

How a baby grows

Over nine months, the **fertilized** cell grows and develops into a tiny human being. Below you can follow a baby's life cycle from the first month to when it is ready to be born.

  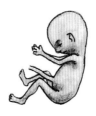  

Month 1 – The baby's heart begins to beat.

Month 2 – The baby has tiny hands and feet.

Month 3 – The baby is fully formed.

Month 4 – The baby grows hair, eyebrows, eyelashes, toenails, and fingernails.

Month 5 – The baby grows quickly, though its head is still much bigger than its body.

 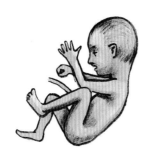  

Month 6 – The baby has a set pattern of sleeping and waking.

Month 7 – The baby moves around in the womb. Its lungs are working.

Month 8 – The baby starts to suck its thumb, ready to suck its mother's milk.

Month 9 – The baby turns head down. It is ready to be born.

28

A baby begins

Like every other person, you started life as a tiny cell. This formed when a **sperm** cell from your father joined with an **ovum** cell from your mother. The fertilized cell began to divide until it formed a ball of cells. Then it embedded itself in the lining of your mother's uterus, or womb, where you received food and **oxygen** through her placenta.

Growing up

In the first two years of life, human beings grow very quickly. At 18 months old, a girl is almost half of her adult height. A boy reaches this stage at about two years old. Human beings then grow steadily until they are about ten, when they shoot up again. Between the ages of 11 and 13, the human body starts to change into an adult. This is called **puberty.** Girls begin to grow breasts and **menstruate.** Boys grow hair on their bodies, and their voices become deeper. The human body stops growing after about 20 years, though it keeps changing as it ages.

Growing old

At about 60 to 70 years old, people begin to show more signs of aging. At this time, it takes longer for the wear and tear on their bodies to be repaired. Skin loses its elastic quality and becomes wrinkled. Hair may turn gray or white as it loses its coloring **pigment.** People also shrink as they grow older because the discs of cartilage between their backbones shrink and their spines become shorter. Today, people with healthy lifestyles live to the age of 80 or 90.

Conclusion

Life cycles of animals and plants are often tied to the changing seasons. Spring is a time when many plants bloom and many animals bear young. In winter, nature is barren and bare. But nature's life cycles continue all the time. **Reproduction** is a part of all these life cycles, and one of the key life processes of all living things. During reproduction, new life is created and a new cycle begins.

Glossary

abdomen   end part of an insect's or arachnid's body

albumen   white of an egg

annual   plant that lives only for a year

asexual reproduction   when something creates new individuals from a single parent dividing in two

breed   to have babies

brood patch   bare patch of skin on a bird's breast for keeping eggs warm during incubation

camouflage   blending in with the surroundings, usually by shape, color, or pattern to be less noticeable

chlorophyll   green coloring found inside plant cells that absorbs energy from sunlight for use in photosynthesis

chrysalis   hard outer case that protects a pupa

cotyledon   seed leaf in which food for the germinating plant is stored

fertile   able to reproduce

fertilization   joining together of a male and female sex cell, or gametes, to produce a new living thing

fungi   large kingdom of living things that obtain energy by decaying or decomposing other living things

gamete   individual male or female sex cell

gene   information in the form of a body chemical, DNA, that carries the instructions for a living thing to develop and survive

genetic   related to genes

germinate   to grow from a seed into a plant

gill   1) thin body part that fish use for breathing   2) fine ridge on the under-side of a mushroom or toadstool's cap where spores grow

glucose   simple sugar in which plants store food

habitat   distinctive type of place or surroundings, such as a woodland, mountain top, grassland, pond, or seashore

incubation period   time in which an animal incubates its eggs

incubate   keeping eggs warm until the young hatch

iodine   type of chemical, found in salt

larva   young form of insect that looks very different from the adults—plural is larvae

marsupials   mammals whose young develop in pouches on the female's body and feed on milk

menstruation   release of a small amount of blood from a woman's body once a month if she releases an egg and the egg is not fertilized

metamorphosis series of changes insects go through as they change from eggs into adults

monotreme mammal that lays eggs

molt to shed a skin and grow another in order to get bigger

nectar sweet, sugary liquid made inside a flower

nucleus rounded structure inside a cell that is the cell's control center—the plural is nuclei

nymph young insect form that looks very much like adults

ovule female sex cell of a plant—after fertilization it becomes a seed

ovum special sex cell, or gamete, made by a female animal

oxygen gas that all living things need to take in to survive

parasite plant or animal that lives on or in anther plant or animal and gets all its food from it

perennial plant that lives for many years

photosynthesis process by which green plants make food from carbon dioxide and water, using energy from sunlight absorbed by their chlorophyll

pigment natural coloring or dye

placental mammal that has young that develop inside the mother's bodies until they are fully formed

pollen tiny grains that are the male sex cells of plants

pollination transfer of pollen from a male flower to a female flower or from the male to female parts of a flower

predator animal that hunts and kills other animals for food

puberty time in girls' and boys' lives when their bodies change from being a child to being an adult

pupa 1) stage in the life cycle of some insects when a larva turns into an adult 2) protective case in which a larva turns into an adult

sexual reproduction creation of new individuals that requires both a male and female parent

spawn 1) another name for the eggs of fish, frogs, and some other animals 2) to lay eggs

species group of organisms that look similar to each other and can breed with each other, but that cannot breed with other things

sperm special sex cell made by a male animal

sporangia structure in ferns where spores are produced.

spore tiny, dust-like speck produced by fungi and many other nonflowering plants that grows into a new plant

yolk yellow part of an egg

zygote cell made when two sex cells join together, which forms the beginning of new life

More Books to Read

Fullick, Ann. *The Living World.* Chicago, Ill.: Heinemann Library, 1999.

Glover, David M. *The Super Science Book of Life Processes.* Austin, Tex.: Raintree Steck-Vaughn, 1994.

Hewitt, Sally. *Life Cycles.* Brookfield, Conn.: Millbrook Press, Inc., 2000.

Index